MODERN SCIENCE
AND ANARCHISM

By

PETER KROPOTKIN

Translated By

DAVID A. MODELL

WITH AN EXCERPT FROM
Comrade Kropotkin
BY VICTOR ROBINSON

First published in 1903

British Library Cataloguing-in-Publication Data
A catalogue record for this book is available
from the British Library

IN LATER LIFE

BY VICTOR ROBINSON

"There are at this moment only two great Russians who think for the Russian people, and those thoughts belong to mankind, - Leo Tolstory and Peter Kropotkin"

— GEORG BRANDES

Such are some of the scenes in the life of Peter Kropotkin- imprisoned by governments, pursued by police, followed by spies, hounded by agents of autocracy.

This peace-loving man whose name is synonym for kindness, this tender soul as modest as Newton, as gentle as Darwin, has been hunted from frontier to border-line. Against none of his persecutors does he utter a single invective. He is the epitome of mildness, the incarnation of humaneness.

Ask anyone who has seen Kropotkin for an hour or has known him for a generation, to describe his most characteristic trait, and the invariable answer will be: simplicity. His is a great spirit— it has cast out flam. "Kropotkin is one of the most sincere and frank of men," says Stepniak. "He always says the truth, pure and simple, without any regard for the *amour propre* of his hearers, or for any consideration whatever. This of his character. Every word he says may be absolutely believed. His sincerity is such, that sometimes in the ardour of discussion an entirely fresh consideration unexpectedly presents itself to his mind, and sets him thinking. He immediately stops, remains quite absorbed for a moment, and then begins to think aloud, speaking as tho he were an opponent. At other times he carries on this discussion mentally, and after moments of silence, turning to his astonished adversary, smilingly says, 'You are right.' This absolute sincerity renders him the best of friends, and gives especial weight to his praise and blame."

AN EXCERPT FROM
Comrade Kropotkin

THE MAN

(1842-1921)

Prince Peter Alexeivitch Kropotkin, revolutionary and scientist, was descended from the old Russian nobility, but decided, at the age of thirty, to throw in his lot with the social rebels not only of his own country, but of the entire world. He became the intellectual leader of Anarchist-Communism; took part in the labor movement; wrote many books and pamphlets; established *Le Révolté* in Geneva and *Freedom* in London; contributed to the *Encyclopedia Britannica*; was twice imprisoned because of his radical activities; and twice visited America. After the Bolshevist revolution he returned to Russia, kept himself apart from Soviet activities, and died true to his ideals.

CONTENTS

TRANSLATOR'S FOREWORD

This translation being submitted in manuscript to the author for approval and criticism, he has returned it with a few brief additions and a number of suggestions. All of the former, of course, are embodied in the text; but of many of the latter I could not avail myself. Instead, before sending the translation to press, I have labored carefully to improve it by making numerous verbal changes calculated to secure greater lucidity and a more correct idiom. In its present form, therefore, the translation is technically unlike that the author has returned to me. Under these circumstances, to have adhered to my intention of displaying "Revised by the Author" on the title-page might prove somewhat misleading. This intention was therefore abandoned. Yet, the author's helpful suggestions and friendly encouragement must be freely acknowledged. It is to do this, and at the same time to absolve him from all responsibility for the translation as it now appears in print, that I make this explanation.

D. A. M.

3

MODERN SCIENCE AND ANARCHISM

I.

Anarchism, like Socialism in general, and like every other social movement, has not, of course, developed out of science or out of some philosophical school. The social sciences are still very far removed from the time when they shall be as exact as are physics and chemistry. Even in meteorology we cannot yet predict the weather a month, or even one week, in advance. It would be unreasonable, therefore, to expect of the young social sciences, which are concerned with phenomena much more complex than winds and rain, that they should foretell social events with any approach to certainty. Besides, it must not be forgotten that men of science, too, are but human, and that most of them either belong by descent to the possessing classes, and are steeped in the prejudices of their class, or else are in the actual service of the government. Not out of the universities, therefore, does Anarchism come.

As Socialism in general, Anarchism was born *among the people;* and it will continue to be full of life and creative power only as long as it remains a thing of the people.

At all times two tendencies were continually at war in human society. On the one hand, the masses were developing, in the form of customs, a number of institutions which were necessary to make social life at all possible—to insure peace amongst men, to settle any disputes that might arise, and to help one another in everything requiring coöperative effort. The savage clan at its earliest stage, the village community, the hunters', and, later on, the industrial guilds, the free town-republics of the middle ages, the beginnings of international law which were worked out in those early periods, and many other institutions,—were elaborated, not by legislators, but by the creative power of the people.

And at all times, too, there appeared sorcerers, prophets, priests, and heads of military organizations, who endeavored to establish and to strengthen their authority over the people. They supported one another, concluded alliances, in order that they might reign over the people, hold them in subjection, and compel them to work for the masters.

Anarchism is obviously the representative of the first tendency—that is, of the creative, constructive power of the people themselves, which aimed at developing institutions of common law in order to protect them from the power-seeking minority. By means of the same popular creative power and constructive activity, based upon modern science and technics, Anarchism tries now as well to develop institutions which would insure a free evolution of society. In this sense, therefore, Anarchists and Governmentalists have existed through all historic times.

Then, again, it always happened also that institutions—even the most excellent so far as their original purpose was concerned, and established originally with the object of securing equality, peace and mutual aid—in the course of time became petrified, lost their original meaning, came under the control of the ruling minority, and became in the end a constraint upon the individual in his endeavors for further development. Then men would rise against these institutions. But, while some of these discontented endeavored to throw off the yoke of the old institutions—of caste, commune or guild—only in order that they themselves might rise over the rest and enrich themselves at their expense; others aimed at a modification of the institutions in the interest of all, and especially in order to shake off the authority which had fixed its hold upon society. All reformers— political, religious, and economic—have belonged to this class. And among them there always appeared persons who, without abiding the time when all their fellow-countrymen, or even a majority of them, shall have become imbued with the same views, moved onward in the struggle against oppression, in mass where it was possible, and single-handed where it could not be done otherwise. These were the revolutionists, and them, too, we meet at all times.

But the revolutionists themselves generally appeared under two different aspects. Some of them, in rising against the established authority, endeavored, not to abolish it, but to take it in their own hands. In place of the authority which had become oppressive, these reformers sought to create a new one, promising that if they exercised it they would have the interests of the people dearly at heart, and would ever represent the people themselves. In this way, however, the authority of the Cæsars was established in Imperial Rome, the power of the Church rose in the first centuries after the fall of the Roman Empire, and the tyranny of dictators grew up in the mediæval communes at the time of their decay. Of the same tendency, too, the kings and the tsars availed themselves to constitute their power at the end of the feudal period. The belief in a popular emperor, that is, Cæsarism, has not died out even yet.

But all the while another tendency was ever manifest. At all times, beginning with Ancient Greece, there were persons and popular movements that aimed, not at the substitution of one government for another, but at the abolition of authority altogether. They proclaimed the supreme rights of the individual and the people, and endeavored to free popular institutions from forces which were foreign and harmful to them, in order that the unhampered creative genius of the people might remould these institutions in accordance with the new requirements. In the history of the ancient Greek republics, and especially in that of the mediæval commonwealths, we find numerous examples of this struggle (Florence and Pskov are especially interesting in this connection). In this sense, therefore, Jacobinists and Anarchists have existed at all times among reformers and revolutionists.

In past ages there were even great popular movements of this latter (Anarchist) character. Many thousands of people then rose against authority—its tools, its courts and its laws—and proclaimed the supreme rights of man. Discarding all written laws, the promoters of these movements endeavored to establish a new society based on equality and labor and on the government of each by his own conscience. In the Christian movement against Roman law, Roman government, and Roman morality (or, rather, Roman immorality), which began in Judea in the reign of Augustus, there undoubtedly existed much that was essentially Anarchistic. Only by degrees it degenerated into an ecclesiastical movement, modeled upon the ancient Hebrew church and upon Imperial Rome itself, which killed the Anarchistic germ, assumed Roman governmental forms, and became in time the chief bulwark of government authority, slavery, and oppression.

Likewise, in the Anabaptist movement (which really laid the foundation for the Reformation) there was a considerable element of Anarchism. But, stifled as it was by those of the reformers who, under Luther's leadership, joined the princes against the revolting peasants, it died out after wholesale massacres of the peasants had been carried out in Holland and Germany. Thereupon the moderate reformers degenerated by degrees into those compromisers between conscience and government who exist to-day under the name of Protestants.

Anarchism, consequently, owes its origin to the constructive, creative activity of the people, by which all institutions of communal life were developed in the past, and to a protest—a revolt against the external force which had thrust itself upon these institutions ; the aim of this protest being to give new scope to the creative activity of the people, in order that it might work out the necessary institutions with fresh vigor.

In our own time Anarchism arose from the same critical and revolutionary protest that called forth Socialism in general. Only that some of the socialists, having reached the negation of Capital and of our social organization based upon the exploitation of labor, went no further. They did not denounce what, in our opinion, constitutes the chief bulwark of Capital ; namely, Government and its chief supports: centralization, law (always written by a minority in the interest of that minority), and Courts of Justice (established mainly for the defence of Authority and Capital).

Anarchism does not exclude these institutions from its criticism. It attacks not only Capital, but also the main sources of the power of Capitalism.

II.

But, though Anarchism, like all other revolutionary movements, was born among the people—in the struggles of real life, and not in the philosopher's studio,—it is none the less important to know what place it occupies among the various scientific and philosophic streams of thought now prevalent : what is its relation to them ; upon which of them principally does it rest ; what method it employs in its researches— in other words, to which school of philosophy of law it belongs, and to which of the now existing tendencies in science it has the greatest affinity.

We have heard of late so much about economic metaphysics that this question naturally presents a certain interest; and I shall endeavor to answer it as plainly as possible, avoiding difficult phraseology wherever it can be avoided.

The intellectual movement of our own times originated in the writings of the Scotch and the French philosophers of the middle and end of the eighteenth century. The universal awakening of thought which began at that time stimulated these thinkers to desire to embody *all* human knowledge in *one* general system. Casting aside mediæval scholasticism and metaphysics, till then supreme, they decided to look upon *the whole* of Nature—the world of the stars, the life of the solar system and of our planet, the development of the animal world and of human societies—as upon phenomena open to scientific investigation and constituting so many branches of natural science.

Freely availing themselves of the truly *scientific*, inductive-deductive method, they approached the study of every group of phenomena—whether of the starry realm, of the animal world, or of the world of human beliefs and institutions—just as the naturalist approaches the study of any physical problem. They carefully investigated the phenomena, and attained their generalizations by means of induction. Deduction helped them in framing certain hypotheses; but these they considered as no more final than, for instance, Darwin regarded his hypothesis concerning the origin of new species by means of the struggle for existence, or Mendeléeff his "periodic law." They saw in these hypotheses suppositions that were very convenient for the classification of facts and their further study, but which were subject to verification by inductive means, and which would become laws—that is, verified generalizations—only after they have stood this test, and after an explanation of cause and effect had been given.

When the centre of the philosophic movement had shifted from Scotland and England to France, the French philosophers, with their natural sense of harmony, betook themselves to a systematic rebuilding of all the human sciences —the natural and the humanitarian sciences— on the same principles. From this resulted their attempt to construct a generalization of all knowledge, that is, a philosophy of the whole world and all its life. To this they endeavored to give a harmonious, scientific form, discarding all metaphysical constructions and explaining all phenomena by the action of the same mechanical forces which had proved adequate to the explanation of the origin and the development of the earth.

It is said that, in answer to Napoleon's remark to Laplace that in his " System of the World " God was nowhere mentioned, Laplace replied,

"I had no need of this hypothesis." But Laplace not only succeeded in writing his work without this supposition: he nowhere in this work resorted to metaphysical entities; to words which conceal a very vague understanding of phenomena and the inability to represent them in concrete material forms—in terms of measurable quantities. He constructed his system without metaphysics. And although in his "System of the World" there are no mathematical calculations, and it is written in so simple a style as to be accessible to every intelligent reader, yet the mathematicians were able subsequently to express every separate thought of this book in the form of an exact mathematical equation— in terms, that is, of measurable quantities. So rigorously did Laplace reason and so lucidly did he express himself.

The French eighteenth-century philosophers did exactly the same with regard to the phenomena of the spiritual world. In their writings one never meets with such metaphysical statements as are found, say, in Kant. Kant, as is well known, explained the moral sense of man by a "categorical imperative" which might at the same time be considered desirable as a universal law.*

---

* Kant's version of the ethical maxim, "Do to others as you would have them do to you," reads: "Act only on that maxim whereby thou canst at the same time will that it should become a universal law."—*Translator.*

But in this dictum every word ("imperative," "categorical," "law," "universal") is a vague verbal substitute for the material fact which is to be explained. The French encyclopædists, on the contrary, endeavored to explain, just as their English predecessors had done, whence came the ideas of good and evil to man, without substituting "a word for the missing conception," as Goethe put it. They took the living man as he is. They studied him and found, as did Hutcheson (in 1725) and, after him, Adam Smith in his best work, " The Theory of Moral Sentiments,"—that the moral sentiments have developed in man from the feeling of pity (sympathy), through his ability to put himself in another's place; from the fact that we almost feel pain and grow indignant when a child is beaten in our presence. From simple observations of common facts like these, they gradually attained to the broadest generalizations. In this manner they actually did explain the complex moral sense by facts more simple, and did not substitute for moral facts well known to and understood by us, obscure terms like "the categorical imperative," or " universal law," which do not explain anything. The merit of such a treatment is self-evident. Instead of the " inspiration from above" and a superhuman, miraculous origin of the moral sense, they dealt with the feeling of pity, of sympathy—derived by man through experience and inheritance, and subsequently perfected by further observation of social life.

When the thinkers of the eighteenth century turned from the realm of stars and physical phenomena to the world of chemical changes, or from physics and chemistry to the study of plants and animals, or from botany and zoölogy to the development of economical and political forms of social life and to religions among men,— they never thought of changing their method of investigation. To all branches of knowledge they applied that same inductive method. And nowhere, not even in the domain of moral concepts, did they come upon any point where this method proved inadequate. Even in the sphere of moral concepts they felt no need of resorting again either to metaphysical suppositions ("God," "immortal soul," "vital force," "a categorical imperative" decreed from above, and the like), or of exchanging the inductive method for some other, scholastic method. They thus endeavored to explain *the whole world—all its phenomena—* in the same natural-scientific way. The encyclopædists compiled their monumental encyclopædia, Laplace wrote his "System of the World," and Holbach " The System of Nature ;" Lavoisier brought forward the theory of the indestructibility of matter, and therefore also of energy or motion (Lomonósoff was at the same

time outlining the mechanical theory of heat *) ;
Lamarck undertook to explain the formation of
new species through the accumulation of varia-
tions due to environment ; Diderot was furnish-
ing an explanation of morality, customs, and
religions requiring no inspiration from without ;
Rousseau was attempting to explain the origin
of political institutions by means of a social con-
tract—that is, an act of man's free will. . . .
In short, there was no branch of science which
the thinkers of the eighteenth century had not
begun to treat on the basis of material phenomena—and all by that same inductive method.

Of course, some palpable blunders were made
in this daring attempt. Where knowledge was
lacking, hypotheses—often very bold, but some-

---

* Readers of Russian literature to whom Lomonósoff
is known only by his literary work, may be surprised as
much as I was to find his name mentioned in connection with the theory of heat. On seeing the name in the
original, I promptly consulted the library—so sure was
I that I was confronted with a typographical error. There
was no mistake, however. For, Mikhail Vassilievich
Lomonósoff (1712-1765), by far the most broadly gifted
Russian of his time, was—I have thus been led to discover—even more ardently devoted to science than to the
muses. His accomplishments in the physical sciences
alone, in which he experimented and upon which he
wrote and lectured extensively, would have won for him
lasting fame in the history of Russian culture and first
mention among its devotees.— *Translator.*

times entirely erroneous—were put forth. But a new method was being applied to the development of all branches of science, and, thanks to it, these very mistakes were subsequently readily detected and pointed out. And at the same time a means of investigation was handed down to our nineteenth century which has enabled us to build up our entire conception of the world upon scientific bases, having freed it alike from the superstitions bequeathed to us and from the habit of disposing of scientific questions by resorting to mere verbiage.

However, after the defeat of the French Revolution, a general reaction set in—in politics, in science, and in philosphy. Of course the fundamental principles of the great Revolution did not die out. The emancipation of the peasants and townspeople from feudal servitude, equality before the law, and representative (constitutional) government, proclaimed by the Revolution, slowly gained ground in and out of France. After the *Revolution*, which had proclaimed the great principles of liberty, equality, and fraternity, a slow *evolution* began—that is, a gradual reorganization which introduced into life and law the principles marked out, but only partly realized, by the Revolution. (Such a realization through evolution of principles proclaimed by the preceding revolution, may even be regarded as a general law of social development). Although the Church, the State, and even Science trampled on the banner upon which the Revolution had inscribed the words "Liberty, Equality, and Fraternity"; although to be reconciled to the existing state of things became for a time a universal watch-word; still the principles of freedom were slowly entering into the affairs of life. It is true that the feudal obligations abolished by the republican armies of Italy and Spain were again restored in these countries, and that even the inquisition itself was revived. But a mortal blow had already been dealt them—and their doom was sealed. The wave of emancipation from the feudal yoke reached, first, Western, and then Eastern Germany, and spread over the peninsulas. Slowly moving eastward, it reached Prussia in 1848, Russia in 1861, and the Balkans in 1878. Slavery disappeared in America in 1863. At the same time the ideas of the equality of all citizens before the law, and of representative government were also spreading from west to east, and by the end of the century Russia alone remained under the yoke of autocracy, already much impaired.

On the other hand, on the threshold of the nineteenth century, the ideas of economic emancipation had already been proclaimed. In England, Godwin published in 1793 his remarkable work, "An Enquiry into Political Justice," in which he was the first to establish the theory of non-governmental socialism, that is, Anarchism ; and Babeuf—especially influenced, as it seems, by Buonarotti—came forward in 1796 as the first theorist of centralized State-socialism.

Then, developing the principles already laid down in the eighteenth century, Fourier, Saint-Simon, and Robert Owen came forward as the three founders of modern socialism in its three chief schools ; and in the forties Proudhon, un-acquainted with the work of Godwin, laid down anew the bases of Anarchism.

The scientific foundations of both govern-mental and non-governmental socialism were thus laid down at the beginning of the nineteenth century with a thoroughness wholly unappre-ciated by our contemporaries. Only in two re-spects, doubtless very important ones, has mod-ern socialism materially advanced. It has be-come revolutionary, and has severed all connec-tion with the Christian religion. It realized that for the attainment of its ideals a Social Revolu-tion is necessary—not in the sense in which peo-ple sometimes speak of an "industrial revolu-tion" or of " a revolution in science," but in the *real*, material sense of the word " Revolution " —in the sense of rapidly changing the funda-mental principles of present society by means which, in the usual run of events, are considered illegal. And it ceased to confuse its views with the optimist reforming tendencies of the Christian religion. But this latter step had already been taken by Godwin and R. Owen. As regards the admiration of centralized authority and the preaching of discipline, for which man is historically indebted chiefly to the mediæval church and to church rule generally—these survivals have been retained among the mass of the State socialists, who have thus failed to rise to the level of their two English forerunners.

·Of the influence which the reaction that set in after the Great Revolution has had upon the development of the sciences, it would be difficult to speak in this essay.* Suffice it to say, that by far the greater part of what modern science prides itself on was already marked out, and more than marked out—sometimes even expressed in a definite scientific form—at the end of the eighteenth century. The mechanical theory of heat and the indestructibility of motion (the conservation of energy); the modification of species by the action of environment; physiological psychology; the anthropological view of history, religion, and legislation; the laws of development of thought—in short, the whole mechanical conception of the world and all the

---

*Something in this line is set forth in my lecture ''On the Scientific Development in the XIX Century.''

elements of a synthetic philosophy (a philosophy which embraces all physical, chemical, living and social phenomena),—were already outlined and partly formulated in the preceding century.

But, owning to the reaction which set in, these discoveries were kept in the background during a full half-century. Men of science suppressed them or else declared them "unscientific." Under the pretext of "studying facts" and "gathering scientific material," even such exact measurements as the determination of the mechanical power necessary for obtaining a given amount of heat (the determination by Séguin and Joule of the mechanical equivalent of heat) were set aside by the scientists. The English Royal Society even declined to publish the results of Joule's investigations into this subject on the ground that they were "unscientific." And the excellent work of Grove upon the unity of physical forces, written in 1843, remained up to 1856 in complete obscurity. Only on consulting the history of the exact sciences can one fully understand the forces of reaction which then swept over Europe.

The curtain was suddenly rent at the end of the fifties, when that liberal, intellectual movement began in Western Europe which led in Russia to the abolition of serfdom, and deposed Schelling and Hegel in philosophy, while in life it called forth the bold negation of intellectual slavery and submission to habit and authority, which is known under the name of Nihilism.

It is interesting to note in this connection the extent to which the socialist teachings of the thirties and forties, and also the revolution of 1848, have helped science to throw off the fetters placed upon it by the post-revolutionary reaction. Without entering here into detail, it is sufficient to say that the above-mentioned Séguin and Augustin Thierry (the historian who laid the foundations for the study of the folk-mote regime and of federalism) were Saint-Simonists, that Darwin's fellow-worker, A. R. Wallace, was in his younger days an enthusiastic follower of Robert Owen; that Auguste Comte was a Saint-Simonist, and Ricardo and Bentham were Owenists; and that the materialists Charles Vogt and George Lewis, as well as Grove, Mill, Spencer, and many others, had lived under the influence of the radical socialstic movement of the thirties and forties. It was to this very influence that they owed their scientific boldness.

The simultaneous appearance of the works of Grove, Joule, Berthollet and Helmholtz; of Darwin, Claude Bernard, Moleschott and Vogt; of Lyell, Bain, Mill and Burnouf —all in the brief space of five or six years (1856–1862),— radically changed the most fundamental views of science. Science suddenly started upon a new path. Entirely new fields of investigation were opened with amazing rapidity. The science of life (Biology), of human institutions (Anthropology), of reason, will and emotions (Psychology), of the history of rights and religions, and so on—grew up under our very eyes, staggering the mind with the boldness of their generalizations and the audacity of their deductions. What in the preceding century was only an ingenious guess, now came forth proved by the scales and the microscope, verified by thousands of applications. The very manner of writing changed, and science returned to the clearness, the precision, and the beauty of exposition which are peculiar to the inductive method and which characterized those of the thinkers of the eighteenth century who had broken away from metaphysics.

To predict what direction science will take in its further development is, evidently, impossible. As long as men of science depend upon the rich and the governments, so long will they of necessity remain subject to influence from this quarter; and this, of course, can again arrest for a time the development of science. But one thing is certain: in the form that science is now assuming there is no longer any need of the hypothesis which Laplace considered useless, or of the metaphysical "words" which Goethe ridiculed. The book of nature, the book of organic life, and that of human development, can already be read without resorting to the power of a creator, a mystical "vital force," an immortal soul, Hegel's trilogy, or the endowment of abstract symbols with real life. Mechanical phenomena, in their ever-increasing complexity, suffice for the explanation of nature and the whole of organic and social life.

There is much, very much, in the world that is still unknown to us—much that is dark and incomprehensible ; and of such unexplained gaps new ones will always be disclosed as soon as the old ones have been filled up. But we do not know of, and do not see the possibility of discovering, any domain in which the phenomena observed in the fall of a stone, or in the impact of two billiard balls, or in a chemical reaction—that is, mechanical phenomena—should prove inadequate to the necessary explanations.

III.

It was natural that, as soon as science had attained such generalizations, the need of *a synthetic philosophy* should be felt; a philosophy which, no longer discussing "the essence of things," "first causes," the "aim of life," and similar symbolic expressions, and repudiating all sorts of anthropomorphism (the endowment of natural phenomena with human characteristics), should be a digest and unification of all our knowledge; a philosophy which, proceeding from the simple to the complex, would furnish a key to the understanding of all nature, in its entirety, and, through that, indicate to us the lines of further research and the means of discovering new, yet unknown, correlations (so-called laws), while at the same time it would inspire us with confidence in the correctness of our conclusions, however much they may differ from current superstitions.

Such attempts at a constructive synthetic philosophy were made several times during the nineteenth century, the chief of them being those of Auguste Comte and of Herbert Spencer. On these two we shall have to dwell.

The need of such a philosophy as this was admitted already in the eighteenth century—by the philosopher and economist Turgot and, subsequently, even more clearly by Saint-Simon. As has been stated above, the encyclopædists, and likewise Voltaire in his "Philosophical Dictionary," had already begun to construct it. In a more rigorous, scientific form which would satisfy the requirements of the exact sciences, it was now undertaken by Auguste Comte.

It is well known that Comte acquitted himself very ably of his task so far as the exact sciences were concerned. He was quite right in including the science of life (Biology) and that of human societies (Sociology) in the circle of sciences compassed by his positive philosophy; and his philosophy has had a great influence upon all scientists and philosophers of the nineteenth century.

But why was it that this great philosopher proved so weak the moment he took up, in his "Positive Politics," the study of social institutions, especially those of modern times? This is the question which most admirers of Comte have asked themselves. How could such a broad and strong mind come to the religion which Comte preached in the closing years of his life? Littré and Mill, it is well known, refused even to recognize Comte's "Politics" as part of his philosophy; they considered it the product of a weakened mind; while others utterly failed in their endeavors to discover a unity of method in the two works.*

* None that know the author's fairness of mind will be likely to accuse him of partiality in the scathing criticism he here makes of the Apostle of Positivism. Lest any reader be inclined to do so, however, it may not be amiss to cite on this point the opinion of a critic unquestionably conservative and, presumably, impartial—an opinion I came upon by mere chance while engaged on this translation. Scattered through pages 560 to 563 of Falckenberg's "History òf Modern Philosophy" (Henry Holt & Co., New York, 1893), I find the follow-

And yet the contradiction between the two parts of Comte's philosophy is in the highest degree characteristic and throws a bright light upon the problems of our own time.

When Comte had finished his "Course of Positive Philosophy," he undoubtedly must have perceived that he had not yet touched upon the most important point—namely, the origin in man of *the moral principle* and the influence of this principle upon human life. He was bound to account for the origin of this principle, to explain it by the same phenomena by which he had explained life in general, and to show why man feels the necessity of obeying his moral sense, or, at least, of reckoning with it. But for this he was lacking in knowledge (at the time he

---

ing estimate of Comte and his uneven work: "The extraordinary character of which [Comte's philosophy] has given occasion to his critics to make a complete division between the second, 'subjective or sentimental,' period of his thinking, in which the philosopher is said to be transformed into the high priest of a new religion, and the first, the positivistic period. . . . Beneath the surface of the most sober inquiry mystical and dictatorial tendencies pulsate in Comte from the beginning. . . . The historical influence exercised by Comte through his later writings is extremely small in comparison with that of his chief work. . . . Comte's school divided into two groups—the apostates, who reject the subjective phase and hold fast to the earlier doctrine, and the faithful."— *Translator.*

wrote this was quite natural) as well as in boldness. So, in lieu of the God of all religions,
whom man must worship and to whom he must
appeal in order to be virtuous, he placed *Humanity*, writ large. To this new idol he ordered
us to pray, that we might develop in ourselves
the moral concept. But once this step had
been taken—once it was found necessary to pay
homage to something standing outside of and
higher than the individual in order to retain
man on the moral path—all the rest followed
naturally. Even the ritualism of Comte's religion moulded itself very naturally upon the model
of all the preceding positive religions.

Once Comte would not admit that everything
that is moral in man grew out of observation of
nature and from the very conditions of men living in societies,—this step was necessary. He
did not see that the moral sentiment in man is
as deeply rooted as all the rest of his physical
constitution inherited by him from his slow
evolution ; that the moral concept in man had
made its first appearance in the animal societies
which existed long before man had appeared
upon earth; and that, consequently, whatever
may be the inclinations of separate individuals,
this concept must persist in mankind as long as the
human species does not begin to deteriorate,—
the anti-moral activity of separate men *inevitably*
calling forth a counter-activity on the part of

those who surround them, just as action causes reaction in the physical world. Comte did not understand this, and therefore he was compelled to invent a new idol—Humanity—in order that it should constantly recall man to the moral path.

Like Saint-Simon, Fourier, and almost all his other contemporaries, Comte thus paid his tribute to the Christian education he had received. Without a struggle of the evil principles with the good—in which the two should be equally matched—and without man's application in prayer to the good principle and its apostles on earth for maintaining him in the virtuous path, Christianty cannot be conceived. And Comte, dominated from childhood by this Christian idea, reverted to it as soon as he found himself face to face with the question of morality and the means of fortifying it in the heart of man.

IV.

But it must not be forgotten that Comte wrote his Positivist Philosophy long before the years 1856–1862, which, as stated above, suddenly widened the horizon of science and the world-concept of every educated man.

The works which appeared in these five or six years have wrought so complete a change in the views on nature, on life in general, and on the life of human societies, that it has no parallel in the whole history of science for the past two thousand years. That which had been but vaguely understood—sometimes only guessed at by the encyclopædists, and that which the best minds in the first half of the nineteenth century had so much difficulty in explaining, appeared now in the full armor of *science*; and it presented itself so thoroughly investigated through the inductive-deductive method that every other method was at once adjudged imperfect, false and —unnecessary.

Let us, then, dwell a little longer upon the results obtained in these years, that we may better appreciate the next attempt at a synthetic philosophy, which was made by Herbert Spencer.

Grove, Clausius, Helmholtz, Joule, and a whole group of physicists and astronomers,— as also Kirchhoff, who discovered the spectro-scopic analysis and gave us the means of de-termining the composition of the most distant stars,—these, in rapid succession at the end of the fifties, proved the unity of nature through-out the inorganic world To talk of certain mysterious, imponderable fluids—calorific, mag-netic, electrical—at once became impossible. It was shown that the mechanical motion of molecules which takes place in the waves of the sea or in the vibrations of a bell or a tuning fork, was adequate to the explanation of all the phenomena of heat, light, electricity and mag-netism ; that we can measure them and weigh their energy. More than this : that in the heavenly bodies most remote from us the same vibration of molecules takes place, with the same effects. Nay, the mass movements of the heavenly bodies themselves, which run through space according to the laws of universal gravitation, represent, in all likelihood, nothing else than the resultants of these vibrations of light and electricity, transmitted for billions and trillions of miles through interstellar space.

The same calorific and electrical vibrations of molecules of matter proved also adequate to explain all chemical phenomena. And then, the very life of plants and animals, in its infinitely varied manifestations, has been found to be nothing else than a continually going on exchange of molecules in that wide range of very complex, and hence unstable and easily decomposed, chemical compounds from which are built the tissues of every living being.

Then, already during those years it was understood—and for the past ten years it has been still more firmly established—that the life of the cells of the nervous system and their property of transmitting vibrations from one to the other, afforded a mechanical explanation of the nervous life of animals. Owing to these investigations, we can now understand, without leaving the domain of purely physiological observations, how impressions and images are produced and retained in the brain, how their mutual effects result in the association of ideas (every new impression awakening impressions previously stored up), and hence also—in thought.

Of course, very much still remains to be done and to be discovered in this vast domain; science, scarcely freed yet from the metaphysics which so long hampered it, is only now beginning to explore the wide field of physical psychology. But the start has already been made, and a solid foundation is laid for further labors. The old-fashioned classification of phenomena into two sets, which the German philosopher Kant endeavored to establish,—one concerned with investigations "in time and space" (the world of physical phenomena) and the other "in time only" (the world of spiritual phenomena),—now falls of itself. And to the question once asked by the Russian physiologist, Setchenov: "By whom and how should psychology be studied?" science has already given the answer: "By physiologists, and by the physiological method." And, indeed, the recent labors of the physiologists have already succeeded in shedding incomparably more light than all the intricate discussions of the metaphysicists, upon the *mechanism of thought;* the awakening of impressions, their retention and transmission.

In this, its chief stronghold, metaphysics was thus worsted. The field in which it considered itself invincible has now been taken possession of by natural science and materialist philosophy, and these two are promoting the growth of knowledge in this direction faster than centuries of metaphysical speculation have done.

In these same years another important step was made. Darwin's book on "The Origin of Species" appeared and eclipsed all the rest.

Already in the last century Buffon (apparently even Linnæus), and on the threshold of the nineteenth century Lamarck, had ventured to maintain that the existing species of plants and animals are not fixed forms; that they are variable and vary continually even now. The very fact of family likeness which exists between groups of forms—Lamarck pointed out—is a proof of their common descent from a common ancestry. Thus, for example, the various forms of meadow buttercups, water buttercups, and all other buttercups which we see on our meadows and swamps, must have been produced by the action of environment upon descendants from one common type of ancestors. Likewise, the present species of wolves, dogs, jackals and foxes did not exist in a remote past, but there was in their stead one kind of animals out of which, under various conditions, the wolves, the dogs, the jackals and the foxes have gradually evolved.

But in the eighteenth century such heresies as these had to be uttered with great circumspection. The Church was still very powerful then, and for such heretical views the naturalist had to reckon with prison, torture, or the lunatic's asylum. The "heretics" consequently were cautious in their expressions. Now, however, Darwin and A. R. Wallace could boldly maintain so great a heresy. Darwin even ventured to declare that man, too, had originated, in the same way of slow physiological evolution, from some lower forms of ape-like animals; that his "immortal spirit" and his "moral soul" are as much a product of evolution as the mind and the moral habits of the ant or of the chimpanzee.

We know what storms then broke out upon Darwin and, especially, upon his bold and gifted disciple, Huxley, who sharply emphasized just those conclusions from Darwin's work which were most dreaded by the clergy. It was a fierce battle, but, owing to the support of the masses of the public, the victory was won, nevertheless, by the Darwinians; and the result was that an entirely new and extremely important science—Biology, the science of life in all its manifestations—has grown up under our very eyes during the last forty years.

At the same time Darwin's work furnished a new key to the understanding of all sorts of phenomena — physical, vital, and social. It opened up a new road for their investigation. The idea of a continuous development (evolution) and of a continual adaptation to changing environment, found a much wider application than the origin of species. It was applied to the study of all nature, as well as to men and their social institutions, and it disclosed in these branches entirely unknown horizons, giving explanations of facts which hitherto had seemed quite inexplicable.

Owing to the impulse given by Darwin's work to all natural sciences, Biology was created, which, in Herbert Spencer's hands, soon explained to us how the countless forms of living beings inhabiting the earth may have developed, and enabled Haeckel to make the first attempt at formulating a genealogy of all animals, man included. In the same way a solid foundation for the history of the development of man's customs, manners, beliefs and institutions was laid down—a history the want of which was strongly felt by the eighteenth century philosophers and by Auguste Comte. At the present time this history can be written without resorting to either the formulæ of Hegelean metapysics or to "innate ideas" and "inspiration from without"—without any of those dead formulæ behind which, concealed by words as by clouds, was always hidden the same ancient ignorance and the same superstition. Owing, on the one hand, to the labors of the naturalists, and, on the other, to those of Henry Maine and his followers, who applied the same inductive method to the study of primitive customs and laws that have grown out of them, it became possible in recent years to place the history of the origin and development of human institutions upon as firm a basis as that of the development of any form of plants or animals.

It would, of course, be extremely unfair to forget the enormous work that was done earlier—already in the thirties—towards the working out of the history of institutions by the school of Augustin Thierry in France, by that of Maurer and the " Germanists " in Germany, and in Russia, somewhat later, by Kostomárov, Belyáev and others. In fact, the principle of evolution had been applied to the study of manners and institutions, and also to languages, from the time of the encyclopædists. But to obtain correct, *scientific deductions* from all this mass of work became possible only when the scientists could look upon the established facts in the same way as the naturalist regards the continuous development of the organs of a plant or of a new species.

The metaphysical formulæ have helped, in their time, to make certain approximate generalizations. Especially did they stimulate the slumbering thought, disturbing it by their vague hints as to the unity of life in nature. At a time when the inductive generalizations of the encyclopædists and their English predecessors were almost forgotten (in the first half of the nineteenth century), and when it required some civic courage to speak of the unity of physical and spiritual nature—the obscure metaphysics still upheld the tendency toward generalization. But those generalizations were established either by means of the dialectic method or by means of a semi-conscious induction, and, therefore, were always characterized by a hopeless indefiniteness. The former kind of generalizations was deduced by means of really fallacious syllogisms—similar to those by which in ancient times certain Greeks used to prove that the planets must move in circles "*because* the circle is the most perfect curve ;" and the meagerness of the premises would then be concealed by misty words, and, worse still, by an obscure and clumsy exposition. As to the semi-conscious inductions which were made here and there, they were based upon a very limited circle of observations —similar to the broad but unwarranted generalization of Weissmann, which have recently created some sensation. Then, as the induction was unconscious, the generalizations were put forth in the shape of hard and fast laws, while in reality they were but simple suppositions—

hypotheses, or beginnings only of generalizations, which, far from being "laws," required yet the very first verification by observation. Finally, all these broad deductions, expressed as they were in most abstract forms—as, for instance, the Hegelean "thesis, antithesis, and synthesis,"— left full play for the individual to come to the most varied and often opposite practical conclusions; so that they could give birth, for instance, to Bakunin's revolutionary enthusiasm and to the Dresden Revolution, to the revolutionary Jacobinism of Marx and to the recognition of the "reasonableness of what exists," which reconciled so many Germans to the reaction then existing—to say nothing of the recent vagaries of the so-called Russian Marxists.

V

Since Anthropology—the history of man's physiological development and of his religious, political ideals, and economic institutions—came to be studied *exactly as all other natural sciences are studied*, it was found possible, not only to shed a new light upon this history, but to divest it for ever of the metaphysics which had hindered this study in exactly the same way as the Biblical teachings had hindered the study of Geology.

It would seem, therefore, that when the construction of a synthetic philosophy was undertaken anew by Herbert Spencer, he should have been able, armed as he was with all the latest conquests of science, to build it without falling into the errors made by Comte in his "Positive Politics." And yet Spencer's synthetic philosophy, though it undoubtedly represents an enormous step in advance (complete as it is without religion and religious rites), still contains in its sociological part mistakes as gross as are found in the former work.

The fact is that, having reached in his analysis the psychology of societies, Spencer did not remain true to his rigorously scientific method, and failed to accept all the conclusions to which it had led him. Thus, for example, Spencer admits that the land ought not to become the property of individuals, who, in consequence of their right to raise rents, would hinder others from extracting from the soil all that could be extracted from it under improved methods of cultivation; or would even simply keep it out of use in the expectation that its market price will be raised by the labor of others. An arrangement such as this he considers inexpedient and full of dangers for society. But, while admitting this in the case of the land, he did not venture to extend this conclusion to all other forms of accumulated wealth—for example, to mines, harbors, and factories.

Or, again, while protesting against the interference of government in the life of society, and giving to one of his books a title which is equivalent to a revolutionary programme, "The Individual vs. The State," he, little by little, under the pretext of the *defensive* activity of the State, ended by reconstructing the State in its entirety,—such as it is to-day, only slightly limiting its attributes.

These and other inconsistencies are probably accounted for by the fact that the sociological part of Spencer's philosophy was formulated in his mind (under the influence of the English radical movement) much earlier than its natural-scientific part—namely, before 1851, when the anthropological investigation of human institutions was still in its rudimentary stage. In consequence of this, Spencer, like Comte, did not take up the investigation of these institutions *by themselves*, without preconceived conclusions. Moreover, as soon as he came in his work to social philosophy—to Sociology—he began to make use of a new method, a most unreliable one—the method of analogies—which he, of course, never resorted to in the study of physical phenomena. This new method permitted him to justify a whole series of preconceived theories. Consequently, we do not possess as yet a philosophy constructed in both its parts—natural sciences and sociology — with the aid of the same scientific method.

Then, Spencer, it must also be added, is the man least suited for the study of primitive insti-

.tutions. In this respect he is distinguished even among the English, who generally do not enter readily into foreign modes of life and thought. "We are a people of Roman law, and the Irish are common-law people: therefore we do not understand each other," a very intelligent Englishman once remarked to me. The history of the Englishmen's relations with the "lower races" is full of like misunderstandings. And we see them in Spencer's writings at every step. He is quite incapable of understanding the customs and ways of thinking of the savage, the "blood revenge" of the Icelandic saga, or the stormy life, filled with struggles, of the mediæval cities. The moral ideas of these stages of civilization are absolutely strange to him; and he sees in them only "savagery," "despotism," and "cruelty."

Finally—what is still more important—Spencer, like Huxley and many others, utterly misunderstood the meaning of "the struggle for existence." He saw in it, not only a struggle between *different* species of animals (wolves devouring rabbits, birds feeding on insects, etc.), but also a desperate struggle for food, for living-room, among the different members *within every species*—a struggle which, in reality, does not assume anything like the proportions he imagined.

How far Darwin himself was to blame for this misunderstanding of the real meaning of the struggle for existence, we cannot discuss here. But certain it is that when, twelve years after " The Origin of Species," Darwin published his " Descent of Man " he already understood struggle for life in a different sense. " Those communities," he wrote in the latter work, " which included the greatest number of the most sympathetic members would flourish best and rear the greatest number of offspring." The chapter devoted by Darwin to this subject could have formed the basis of an entirely different and most wholesome view of nature and of the development of human societies (the significance of which Goethe had already foreseen). But it passed unnoticed. Only in 1879 do we find, in a lecture by the Russian zoölogist Kessler, a clear understanding of mutual aid and the struggle for life. " For the *progressive* development of a species," Kessler pointed out, citing several examples, " *the law of mutual aid* is of far greater importance than the law of mutual struggle." Soon after this Louis Büchner published his book " Love," in which he showed the importance of *sympathy* among animals for the development of moral concepts; but, in introducing the idea of love and sympathy instead of simple sociability, he needlessly limited the sphere of his investigations.

To prove and further to develop Kessler's excellent idea, extending it to man, was an easy step. If we turn our minds to a close observation of nature and to an unprejudiced history of human institutions, we soon discover that Mutual Aid really appears, not only as the most powerful weapon in the struggle for existence against the hostile forces of nature and all other enemies, but also as the chief factor of *progressive evolution*. To the weakest animals it assures longevity (and hence an accumulation of mental experience), the possibility of rearing its progeny, and intellectual progress. And those animal species among which Mutual Aid is practiced most, not only succeed best in getting their livelihood, but also stand at the head of their respective class (of insects, birds, mammals) as regards the superiority of their physical and mental development.

This fundamental fact of nature Spencer did not perceive. The struggle for existence within every species, the "free fight" for every morsel of food, Tennyson's "Nature, red in tooth and claw with ravine"—he accepted as a fact requiring no proof, as an axiom. Only in recent years did he begin in some degree to understand the meaning of mutual aid in the animal world, and to collect notes and make experiments in this direction. But even then he still thought of primitive man as of a beast who lived only by snatching, with tooth and claw, the last morsel of food from the mouth of his fellowmen.

Of course, having based the sociological part of his philosophy on so false a premise, Spencer was no longer able to build up the sociological part of his synthetic philosophy without falling into a series of errors.

VI.

In these erroneous views, however, Spencer does not stand alone. Following Hobbes, all the philosophy of the nineteenth century continues to look upon the savages as upon bands of wild beasts which lived an isolated life and fought among themselves over food and wives, until some benevolent authority appeared among them and forced them to keep the peace. Even such a naturalist as Huxley advocated the same views as Hobbes, who maintained that in the beginning people lived in a state of war, fighting "each against all," * till, at last, owing to a few advanced persons of the time, the "first society" was created (see his article "The Struggle for Existence—a Law of Nature.") Even Huxley, therefore, failed to realize that it was not Man who created society, but that social life existed among animals much earlier than the advent of man. Such is the power of deep-rooted prejudice.

---

*Hobbes' exact words are : "Bellum omnium contra omnes." (The war of everyone against everybody). —*Translator.*

45

Were we, however, to trace the history of this prejudice, it would not be difficult to convince ourselves that it originated chiefly in religions and among their representatives. The secret leagues of sorcerers, rain-makers, and so on, among primitive clans, and later on, the Babylonian, Assyrian, Egyptian, Indian, Hebrew and other priesthoods, and later still the Christian priests, have always been endeavoring to persuade men that they lay deep in sin , and that only the intercession of the shaman, the magician, and the priest can keep the evil spirit from assuming control over man, or can prevail with a revengeful God not to visit upon man his retribution for sin. Primitive Christianity, it is true, faintly attempted to break up this prejudice ; but the Christian Church, adhering to the very language of the gospels concerning '' eternal fire '' and " the wrath of God," intensified it still more. The very conception of a son of God who had come to die for "the redemption of sin," served as a basis for this view. No wonder that later on " the Holy Inquisition " subjected people to the most cruel tortures and burned them slowly at the stake in order to afford them an opportunity of repenting and of saving themselves thereby from eternal torment. And not the Catholic Church alone, but all other Christian Churches vied with one another in inventing all kinds of tortures in order to better people "steeped in sin." Up to the present time, nine hundred and ninety-nine persons in a thousand still believe that natural calamities—droughts, floods, earthquakes, and epidemic diseases—are sent by a Divine Being for the purpose of recalling sinful mankind to the right path. In this belief an enormous majority of our children are being brought up to this very day.

At the same time the State, in its schools and universities, countenances the same belief in the innate perversity of man. To prove the necessity of some power that stands above society and inculcates in it the moral principles (with the aid of punishments inflicted for violations of "moral law," for which, by means of a clever trick, the written law is easily substituted),—to keep people in this belief is a matter of life or death to the State. Because, the moment people come to doubt the necessity and possibility of such an inoculation of morality, they will begin to doubt the higher mission of their rulers as well.

In this way everything — our religious, our historical, our legal, and our social education— is imbued with the idea that man, left to himself, would soon turn into a beast. If it were not for the authority exercised over them, people would devour one another; nothing but brutality and war of each against all can be expected from "the mob." It would perish, if

the policeman, the sheriff and the hangman—
the chosen few, the salt of the earth—did not
tower above it and interpose to prevent the universal free-fight, to educate the people to respect
the sanctity of law and discipline, and with a
wise hand lead them onward to those times
when better ideas shall find a nestling place in
the "uncouth hearts of men" and render the
rod, the prison, and the gallows less necessary
than they are at present.

We laugh at a certain king who, on going
into exile in 1848, said: "My poor subjects;
now they will perish without me!" We smile
at the English clerk who believes that the
English are the lost tribe of Israel, appointed
by God himself to administer good government to "all other, lower races." But does not
the great majority of fairly educated people
among all nations entertain the same exalted
opinion with regard to itself?

And yet, a scientific study of the development of human society and institutions leads to
an entirely different conclusion. It shows that
the habits and customs for mutual aid, common
defence, and the preservation of peace, which were
established since the very first stages of human
pre-historic times—and which alone made it
possible for man, under very trying natural conditions, to survive in the struggle for existence,—

that these social conventions have been worked out precisely by this anonymous "mob." As to the so-called "leaders" of humanity, they have not contributed anything useful that was not developed previously in customary law; they may have emphasized (they nearly always vitiated) some useful existing customs, but they have not invented them; while they always strove, on their side, to turn to their own advantage the common-law institutions that had been worked out by the masses for their mutual protection, or, failing in this, endeavored to destroy them.

Even in the remotest antiquity, which is lost in the darkness of the stone age, men already lived in societies. In these societies was already developed a whole network of customs and sacred, religiously-respected institutions of the communal regime or of the clan which rendered social life possible. And through all the subsequent stages of development we find it was exactly this constructive force of the "uninformed mob" that worked out new modes of life and new means for mutual support and the maintenance of peace, as new conditions arose.

On the other hand, modern science has proved conclusively that Law—whether proclaimed as the voice of a divine being or proceeding from the wisdom of a lawgiver—never did anything else than prescribe already existing, useful habits and customs, and thereby hardened them into unchangeable, crystallized forms. And in doing this it always added to the "useful customs," generally recognized as such, a few new rules—in the interest of the rich, warlike and armed minority. "Thou shalt not kill," said the Mosaic law, "Thou shalt not steal," "Thou shalt not bear false witness," and then it added to these excellent injunctions: "Thou shalt not covet thy neighbor's wife, his slave, nor his ass," which injunction legalized slavery for all time and put woman on the same level as a slave and a beast of burden.

"Love your neighbor," said Christianity later on, but straightway added, in the words of Paul the Apostle: "Slaves, be subject to your masters," and "There is no authority but from God,"—thereby emphasizing the division of society into slaves and masters and sanctifying the authority of the scoundrels who reigned at Rome. The Gospels, though teaching the sublime idea of "no punishment for offences," which is, of course, the essence of Christianity— the token which differentiates it and Buddhism from all other positive religions—speak at the same time all the while about an avenging God who takes his revenge even upon children, thus necessarily impressing upon mankind the opposite idea of *vengeance*.

We see the same thing in the laws of the so-called "Barbarians," that is, of the Gauls, the Lombards, the Allemains, and the Saxons, when these people lived in their communities, free from the Roman yoke. The Barbarian codes converted into law an undoubtedly excellent custom which was then in process of formation : the custom of paying a penalty for wounds and killing, instead of practicing the law of retaliation (an eye for an eye, a tooth for a tooth, wound for wound, and death for death). But at the same time they also legalized and perpetuated the division of freemen into classes—a division which only then began to appear. They exacted from the offender varying compensations, according as the person killed or wounded was a freeman, a military man, or a king (the penalty in the last case being equivalent to life-long servitude). The original idea of this scale of compensations to be paid to the wronged family according to its social position, was evidently that a king's family, which loses more than the family of an ordinary freeman by being deprived of its head, was entitled to receive a greater compensation. But the law, by restating the custom, legalized for all time the division of people into classes— and so legalized it that up to the present, a thousand years since, we have not got rid of it.

And this happened with the legislation of every age, down to our own time. The oppression of the preceding epoch was thus transmitted by law from the old society to the new, which grew up upon the ruins of the old. The oppression of the Persian empire passed on to Greece; the oppression of the Macedonian empire, to Rome; the oppression and cruelty of the Roman empire, to the mediæval European States then just arising.

Every social safeguard, all forms of social life in the tribe, the commune, and the early mediæval town-republics; all forms of intertribal, and later on inter-provincial, relations, out of which international law was subsequently evolved; all forms of mutual support and all institutions for the preservation of peace—including the jury,—were developed by the creative genius *of the anonymous masses.* While all the laws of every age, down to our own, always consisted of the same two elements: one which fixed and crystallized certain forms of life that were universally recognized as useful; the other which was a superstructure—sometimes even nothing but a cunning clause adroitly smuggled in in order to establish and strengthen the growing authority of the nobles, the king, and the priest—to give it sanction.

So, at any rate, we are led to conclude by the scientific study of the development of human society, upon which for the last thirty years not a few conscientious men of science have labored.

They themselves, it is true, seldom venture to express such heretical conclusions as those stated above. But the thoughtful reader inevitably comes to them on reading their works.

VII.

What position, then, does Anarchism occupy in the great intellectual movement of the nineteenth century?

The answer to this question has already been partly formulated in the preceding pages. Anarchism is a world-concept based upon a mechanical explanation of all phenomena,* embracing the whole of Nature—that is, including in it the life of human societies and their economic, political, and moral problems. Its method of investigation is that of the exact natural sciences, by which every scientific conclusion must be verified. Its aim is to construct a synthetic philosophy comprehending in one generalization all the phenomena of Nature—and therefore also the life of societies,—avoiding, however, the errors mentioned above into which, for the reasons there given, Comte and Spencer had fallen.

It is therefore natural that to most of the questions of modern life Anarchism should give

---

* It were more correct to say, a *kinetic* explanation, but this word is not so commonly known.

new answers, and hold with regard to them a position differing from those of all political and, to a certain extent, of all socialistic parties, which have not yet freed themselves from the metaphysical fictions of old.

Of course, the elaboration of a complete mechanical world-conception has hardly been begun in its sociological part—in that part, that is, which deals with the life and the evolution of societies. But the little that has been done undoubtedly bears a marked—though often not fully conscious—character. In the domain of philosophy of law, in the theory of morality, in political economy, in history (both of nations and institutions), Anarchism has already shown that it will not content itself with metaphysical conclusions, but will seek in every case a natural-scientific basis. It rejects the metaphysics of Hegel, of Schelling, and of Kant ; it disowns the commentators of Roman and Canon Law, together with the learned apologists of the State ; it does not consider metaphysical political economy a science ; and it endeavors to gain a clear comprehension of every question raised in these branches of knowledge, basing its investigations upon the numerous researches that have been made during the last thirty or forty years from a naturalist point of view.

In the same way as the metaphysical conceptions of a Universal Spirit, or of a Creative Force in Nature, the Incarnation of the Idea, Nature's Goal, the Aim of Existence, the Unknowable, Mankind (conceived as having a separate spiritualized existence), and so on—in the same way as all these have been brushed aside by the materialist philosophy of to-day, while the embryos of generalizations concealed beneath these misty terms are being translated into the concrete language of natural sciences,—so we proceed in dealing with the facts of social life. Here also we try to sweep away the metaphysical cobwebs, and to see what embryos of generalizations—if any—may have been concealed beneath all sorts of misty words.

When the metaphysicians try to convince the naturalist that the mental and moral life of man develops in accordance with certain " Immanent (in-dwelling) Laws of the Spirit," the latter shrugs his shoulders and continues his physiological study of the mental and moral phenomena of life, with a view to showing that they can all be resolved into chemical and physical phenomena. He endeavors to discover the natural laws on which they are based. Similarly, when the Anarchists are told, for instance, that—as Hegel says—every development consists of a Thesis, an Antithesis, and a Synthesis; or that "the object of Law is the establishment of Justice, which represents the realization of the Highest Idea;"

or, again, when they are asked,—What, in their opinion, is "the Object of Life?" they, too, simply shrug their shoulders and wonder how, at the present state of development of natural science, old fashioned people can still be found who continue to believe in "words" like these and still express themselves in the language of primitive anthropomorphism (the conception of nature as of a thing governed by a being endowed with human attributes). High-flown words do not scare the Anarchists, because they know that these words simply conceal either ignorance—that is, uncompleted investigation—or, what is much worse, mere superstition. They therefore pass on and continue their study of past and present social ideas and institutions according to the scientific method of induction. And in doing so they find, of course, that the development of social life is incomparably more complicated—and incomparably more interesting for practical purposes—than it would appear from such formulæ.

We have heard much of late about "the dialectic method," which was recommended for formulating the socialist ideal. Such a method we do not recognize, neither would the modern natural sciences have anything to do with it. "The dialectic method" reminds the modern naturalist of something long since passed—of something outlived and now happily forgotten by science.

The discoveries of the nineteenth century in mechanics, physics, chemistry, biology, physical psychology, anthropology, psychology of nations, etc., were made—*not by the dialectic method, but by the natural-scientific method, the method of induction and deduction.* And since man is part of nature, and since the life of his "spirit"—personal as well as social—is just as much a phenomenon of nature as is the growth of a flower or the evolution of social life amongst the ants and the bees,—there is no cause for suddenly changing our method of investigation when we pass from the flower to man, or from a settlement of beavers to a human town.

The inductive-deductive method has proved its merits so well, in that the nineenth century, which has applied it, has caused science to advance more in a hundred years than it had advanced during the two thousand years that went before. And when, in the second half of the century, this method began to be applied to the investigation of human society, no point was ever reached where it was found necessary to abandon it and again adopt mediæval scholasticism—as revised by Hegel. Besides, when, for example, philistine naturalists, seemingly basing their arguments on "Darwinism," began to teach, "Crush everyone weaker than yourself; such is the law of nature," it was easy for us to prove by the same scientific method that no such law exists : that the life of animals teaches us something entirely different, and that the conclusions of the philistines were absolutely un-scientific. They were just as unscientfic as, for instance, the assertion that the inequality of wealth is a law of nature, or that capitalism is the most convenient form of social life cal-culated to promote progress. Precisely this natural-scientific method, applied to economic facts, enables us to prove that the so-called "laws" of middle-class sociology, including also their political economy, are not laws at all, but simply guesses, or mere assertions which have never been verified at all. Moreover, every investigation bears fruit only when it has a definite aim—when it is undertaken for the purpose of obtaining an answer to a definite and clearly worded question. And it is the more fruitful the more clearly the explorer sees the connection that exists between his problem and his general concept of the universe—the place which the former occupies in the latter. The better he understands the importance of the problem in the general concept, the easier will the answer be. The question, then, which Anarchism puts to itself may be stated thus : "What forms of social life assure to a given society, and then to mankind generally, the greatest amount of happiness, and hence also of vitality ? " " What forms of social life allow this amount of happiness to grow and to develop, quantitatively as well as qualitatively,— that is, to become more complete and more varied?" (from which, let us note in passing, a definition of *progress* is derived). The desire to promote evolution in this direction determines the scientific as well as the social and artistic activity of the Anarchist.

VIII.

Anarchism originated, as has already been said, from the demands of practical life.

At the time of the great French Revolution of 1789–1793, Godwin had the opportunity of himself seeing how the governmental authority created during the revolution itself acted as a retarding force upon the revolutionary movement. And he knew, too, what was then taking place in England, under cover of Parliament (the confiscation of public lands, the kidnapping of poor workhouse children by factory agents and their deportation to weavers' mills, where they perished wholesale, and so on). He understood that the government of the "One and Undivided" Jacobinist Republic would not bring about the necessary revolution; that the revolutionary government itself, from the very fact of its being a guardian of the State, was an obstacle to emancipation; that to insure the success of the revolution, people ought to part, first of all, with their belief in Law, Authority, Uniformity, Order, Property, and other superstitions inherited by us from our servile past. And with this purpose in view he wrote "Political Justice."

The theorist of Anarchism who followed Godwin, Proudhon, had himself lived through the Revolution of 1848 and had seen with his own eyes the crimes perpetrated by the revolutionary republican government, and the inapplicability of the State Socialism of Louis Blanc. Fresh from the impressions of what he had witnessed, Proudhon penned his admirable works, "A General Idea of the Social Revolution " and " Confessions of a Revolutionist," in which he boldly advocated the abolition of the State and proclaimed Anarchy.

And finally, the idea of Anarchism reappeared again in the International Working Men's Association, after the revolution that was attempted in the Paris Commune of 1871. The complete failure of the Council of the Commune and its incapacity to act as a revolutionary body—although it consisted, in due proportion, of representatives of every revolutionary faction of the time (Jacobinists, the followers of Louis Blanc, and members of the International Working Men's Association), and, on the other hand, the incapacity of the London General Council of the International and its ludicrous and even harmful pretenison to direct the Paris insurrection by orders sent from England,—opened the eyes of many. They forced many members of the International, including Bakunin, to reflect upon the harmfulness of all sorts of government—even such as had been freely elected in the Commune and in the International Working Men's Association. A few months later, the resolution passed by the same general Council of the Association, at a secret conference held in London in 1871 instead of an annual congress, proved still more the inconvenience of having a government in the International. By this dire resolution they decided to turn the entire labor movement into another channel and to convert it from an economic revolutionary movement—from a direct struggle of the working men's organizations against capitalism—into an elective parliamentary and political movement. This decision led to open revolt on the part of the Italian, Spanish, Swiss, and partly also of the Belgian, Federations against the London General Council, out of which movement modern Anarchism subsequently developed.

Every time, then, the anarchist movement sprang up in response to the lessons of actual life and originated from the practical tendencies of events. And, under the impulse thus given it, Anarchism set to work out its theoretic, scientific basis.

No struggle can be successful if it is an un-conscious one, and if it does not render itself a clear and concise account of its aim. No destruction of the existing order is possible, if at the time of the overthrow, or of the struggle leading to the overthrow, the idea of what is to take the place of what is to be destroyed is not always present in the mind. Even the theoretical criticism of the existing conditions is impossible, unless the critic has in his mind a more or less distinct picture of what he would have in place of the existing state. Consciously or unconsciously, *the ideal* of something better is forming in the mind of every one who criticises social institutions.

This is even more the case with a man of action. To tell people, "First let us abolish autocracy or capitalism, and then we will discuss what to put in its place," means simply to deceive oneself and others. And *power* is never created by deception. The very man who speaks thus surely has some idea of what will take the place of the institutions destroyed. Among those who work for the abolition—let us say, of autocracy—some inevitably think of a constitution like that of England or Germany, while others think of a republic, either placed under the powerful dictatorship of their own party or modeled after the French empire-republic, or, again, of a federal republic like that of the United States or Switzerland; while others again strive to achieve a still greater limitation of government authority; a still greater independence of the towns, the communes, the working men's associations, and all other groups united among themselves by free agreements.

Every party thus has its ideal of the future, which serves it as a criterion in all events of political and economic life, as well as a basis for determining its proper modes of action. Anarchism, too, has conceived its own ideal; and this very ideal has led it to find its own immediate aims and its own methods of action different from those of all other political parties and also, to some extent, from those of the socialist parties, which have retained the old Roman and ecclesiastic ideals of governmental organization.

IX.

This is not the place to enter into an exposition of Anarchism. The present sketch has its own definite aim—that of indicating the relation of Anarchism to modern science,—while the fundamental views of Anarchism may be found stated in a number of other works. But two or three illustrations will help us to define the exact relation of our views to modern science and the modern social movement.

When, for instance, we are told that Law (written large) "is the objectification of Truth;" or that "the principles underlying the development of Law are the same as those underlying the development of the human spirit;" or that "Law and Morality are identical and differ only formally;" we feel as little respect for these assertions as does Mephistopheles in Goethe's "Faust." We are aware that those who make such seemingly profound statements as these have expended much thought upon these questions. But they have taken a wrong path; and hence we see in these high-flown sentences mere attempts at unconscious generalization, based upon inadequate foundations and confused, moreover, by words of hypnotic power. In olden times they tried to give "Law" a divine origin; later they began to seek a metaphysical basis for it; now, however, we are able to study its anthropological origin. And, availing ourselves of the results obtained by the anthropological school, we take up the study of social customs, beginning with those of the primitive savages, and trace the origin and the development of the laws at different epochs.

In this way we come to the conclusion already expressed on a preceding page—namely, that all laws have a two-fold origin, and in this very respect differ from those institutions established by custom which are generally recognized as the moral code of a given society. Law confirms and crystallizes these customs, but, while doing so, it takes advantage of this fact to establish (for the most part in a disguised form) the germs of slavery and class distinction, the authority of priest and warrior, serfdom and various other institutions, in the interest of the armed and would-be ruling minority. In this way a yoke has imperceptibly been placed upon man, of which he could only rid himself by means of subsequent bloody revolutions. And this is the course of events down to the present moment—even in contemporary "labor legislation" which, along with "protection of labor," covertly introduces the idea of *compulsory* State arbitration in case of strikes,* a *compulsory* eight-hour day for the workingman (no less than eight hours), military exploitation of the railroads during strikes, legal sanction for the dispossession of the peasants in Ireland, and so on. And this will continue to be so as long as *one* portion of society goes on framing laws for *all* society, and thereby strengthens the power of the State, which forms the chief support of Capitalism.

It is plain, therefore, why Anarchism—which aspires to *Justice* (a term synonymous with

---

* "Compulsory arbitration"—What a glaring contradiction!

equality) more than any lawgiver in the world—has from the time of Godwin rejected all written *laws*.

When, however, we are told that by rejecting Law we reject all morality—since we deny the "categoric imperative" of Kant,—we answer that the very wording of this objection is to us strange and incomprehensible.* It is as strange and incomprehensible to us as it would be to every naturalist engaged in the study of the phenomena of morality. In answer to this argument, we ask : "What do you really mean? Can you not translate your statements into comprehensible language—for instance, as Laplace translated the formulæ of higher mathematics into a language accessible to all, and as all great men of science did and do express themselves?"

Now, what does a man who takes his stand on "universal law" or "the categorical imperative" really mean? Does he mean that *there is* in all men the conception that one ought not to do to another what he would not have done to himself—that it would be better even to return good for evil? If so, well and good. Let us, then, study (as Adam Smith and Hutcheson have already studied) the origin of these

---

* I am not quoting an imaginary example, but one taken from correspondence which I have recently carried on with a German doctor of law.

moral ideas in man, and their course of development. Let us extend our studies also to pre-human times (a thing Smith and Hutcheson could not do). Then, we may analyze to what extent the idea of *Justice* implies that of *Equality*. The question is an important one, because only those who regard *others* as their equals can accept the rule, "Do not to others what you would not have done to yourself." The landlord and the slave-owner, who did not look upon "the serf" and the negro as their equals, did not recognize "the categorical imperative" and "the universal law" as applicable to these unhappy members of the human family. And then, if this observation of ours be correct, we shall see whether it is at all possible to inculcate morality while teaching the doctrine of inequality.

We shall finally analyze, as Mark Guyau did, the facts of self-sacrifice. And then we shall consider what has most promoted the development in man of moral feelings—first, of those which are intimately connected with the idea of equality, and then of the others ; and after this consideration we shall be able to deduce from our study exactly what social conditions and what institutions promise the best results for the future. Is this development promoted by religion, and to what extent? Is it promoted by inequality— economic and political—and by a division into classes? Is it promoted by law? By punishment? By prisons? By the judge? The jailer? The hangman?

Let us study all this in detail, and then only may we speak again of Morality and moralization by means of laws, law courts, jailers, spies, and police. But we had better give up using the sonorous words which only conceal the superficiality of our semi-learning. In their time the use of these words was, perhaps, unavoidable—their application could never have been useful; but now that we are able to approach the study of burning social questions in exactly the same manner as the gardener and the physiologist take up the study of the conditions most favorable for the growth of a plant—let us do so!

Likewise, when certain economists tell us that "in a perfectly free market the price of commodities is measured by the amount of labor socially necessary for their production," we do not take this assertion on faith because it is made by certain authorities or because it may seem to us "tremendously socialistic." It may be so, we say. But do you not notice that by this very statement you maintain that value and the necessary labor *are proportional to each other*—just as the speed of a falling body is proportional to the number of seconds it has been falling ? Thus you maintain a *quantitative relation* between these two magnitudes ; whereas a quantitative relation can be proved *only* by quantitative measurements. To confine yourself to the remark that the exchange-value of commodities "generally" increases when a greater expenditure of labor is required, and then to assert that *therefore* the two quantities are proportional to each other, is to make as great a mistake as the man who would assert that the quantity of rainfall is measured by the fall of the barometer below its average height. He who first observed that, generally speaking, when the barometer is falling a greater amount of rain falls than when it is rising ; or, that there is a certain relation between the speed of a falling stone and the height from which it fell —that man surely made a scientific discovery. But the person who would come after him and assert that the amount of rainfall is *measured* by the fall of the barometer below its average height, or that the space through which a falling body has passed is *proportional* to the time of fall and is measured by it,—that person would not only talk nonsense, but would prove by his very words that the method of scientific research is absolutely strange to him ; that his work is unscientific, full as it may be of scientific expressions. The absence of data is, clearly, no excuse. Hundreds, if not thousands, of similar relationships are known to science in which we see the dependence of one magnitude upon another—for example, the recoil of a cannon depending upon the quantity of powder in the charge, or the growth of a plant depending upon the amount of heat or light received by it; but no scientific man will presume to affirm the proportionality of these magnitudes without having investigated their relations quantitatively, and still less would he represent this proportionality as a scientific *law*. In most instances the dependence is very complex—as it is, indeed, in the theory of value. The necessary amount of labor and value are by no means proportional.

The same remark refers to almost every economic doctrine that is current to-day in certain circles and is being presented with wonderful naivety as an invariable law. We not only find most of these so-called laws grossly erroneous, but maintain also that those who believe in them will themselves become convinced of their error as soon as they come to see the necessity of verifying their quantitative deductions by quantitative investigation.

Moreover, the whole of political economy appears to us in a different light from that in which it is seen by modern economists of both the middle-class and the social-democratic camps. The scientific method (the method of natural scientific induction) being utterly unknown to them, they fail to give themselves any definite account of what constitutes "a law of nature," although they delight in using the term. They do not know—or if they know they continually forget —that every law of nature has a *conditional* character. It is always expressed thus: "*If* certain conditions in nature meet, certain things will happen." "*If* one line intersects another, forming right angles on both sides of it, the consequences will be these or those." *If* two bodies are acted upon by such movements only as exist in interstellar space, and there is no third body within measurable distance of them, then their centres of gravity will approach each other at a certain speed (the law of gravitation)." And so on. In every case there is an "*if*"—a condition.

In consequence of this, all the so-called laws and theories of political economy are in reality no more than statements of the following nature: "Granting that there are always in a country a considerable number of people who cannot subsist a month, or even a fortnight, without accepting the conditions of work imposed upon them by the State, or offered to them by those whom the State recognizes as owners of land, factories, railways, etc., then the results will be so and so."

So far middle-class political economy has

been only an enumeration of what happens under the just-mentioned conditions—without distinctly stating the conditions themselves. And then, having described *the facts* which arise in our society under these conditions, they represent to us these *facts* as rigid, *inevitable economic laws.* As to socialist political economy, although it criticises some of these deductions, or explains others somewhat differently,—it has not yet been original enough to find a path of its own. It still follows in the old grooves, and in most cases repeats the very same mistakes.

And yet, in our opinion, political economy must have an entirely different problem in view. It ought to occupy with respect to human societies a place in science similar to that held by physiology in relation to plants and animals. It must become *the physiology of society.* It should aim at *studying the needs of society and the various means, both hitherto used and available under the present state of scientific knowledge, for their satisfaction.* It should try to analyze how far the present means are expedient and satisfactory, economic or wasteful ; and then, since the ultimate end of every science (as Bacon had already stated) is obviously its practical application to life, it should concern itself with the discovery of means *for the satisfaction of these needs with the smallest possible waste of labor and with the greatest benefit to mankind in general.* Such means would be, in fact, mere corollaries from the relative investigation mentioned above, provided this last had been made on scientific lines.

It will be clear, even from the hasty hints given already, why it is that we come to conclusions so different from those of the majority of economists, both of the middle class and the social-democratic schools ; why we do not regard as "laws" certain of the temporary relations pointed out by them ; why we expound socialism entirely differently ; and why, after studying the tendencies and developments in the economic life of different nations, we come to such radically different conclusions as regards that which is desirable and possible ; why we come to Free Communism, while the majority of socialists arrive at State-capitalism and Collectivism.

Perhaps we are wrong and they are right. But in order to ascertain who is right, it will not do either to quote this and that authority, to refer to Hegel's trilogy, or to argue by the "dialectic method." This question can be settled only by taking up the study of economic relations as facts of natural science.*

---

* A few extracts from a letter written by a renowned Belgian biologist and received when these lines were in print, will help me to make my meaning clearer by a living illustration. The letter was not intended for publication,

Pursuing the same method, Anarchism arrives also at its own conclusions concerning the State. It could not rest content with current metaphysical assertions like the following:

and therefore I do not name its author: "The further I read [such and such a work]—he writes—the surer I become that nowadays only those are capable of studying economic and social questions who have studied the natural sciences and *have become imbued with their spirit.* Those who have received only a so-called classical education are no longer able to understand the present intellectual movement and are equally incapable of studying a mass of social questions. . . . . The idea of the integration of labor and of *division of labor in time only* [the idea that it would be expedient for society to have every person cultivating the land and following industrial and intellectual pursuits in turn, thus varying his labor and becoming a variously-developed individual] will become in time one of the cornerstones of economic science. A number of biological facts are in harmony with the thought just underlined, which shows that we are here dealing with a law of nature [that in nature, in other words, an economy of forces may frequently result in this way]. If we examine the vital functions of any living being at different periods of its life, and even at different times of the year, and sometimes at different moments of the day, we find the application of the division of labor in time, which is inseparably connected with the division of labor among the different organs (the law of Adam Smith).

"Scientific people unacquainted with the natural sciences, are frequently unable to understand the true meaning of *a law* of nature; the word *law* blinds them,

" The State is the affirmation of the idea of the highest Justice in Society ; " or " The State is the instigation and the instrument of progress ; " or, "without the State, Society is impossible." Anarchism has approached the study of the State exactly in the manner the naturalist approaches the study of social life among bees and ants, or among the migratory birds which hatch their young on the shores of sub-arctic lakes. It would be useless to repeat here the conclusions to which this study has brought us with reference to the history of the different political forms (and to their desirable or probable evolu-

---

and they imagine that laws, like that of Adam Smith, have a fatalistic power from which it is impossible to rid oneself. When they are shown the *reverse* side of this last—the sad results of individualism, from the point of view of development and personal happiness,—they answer : *this is an inexorable law*, and sometimes they give this answer so off-handedly that they thereby betray their belief in a kind of infallibility. The naturalist, however, knows that science can paralyze the harmful consequences of a *law ;* that frequently he who goes against nature wins the victory.

''The force of gravity compels bodies *to fall*, but it also compels the balloon *to rise*. *To us* this seems so clear ; but the economists of the classical school appear to find it difficult to understand the full meaning of this observation.

''*The law of the division of labor in time* will counterbalance the law of Adam Smith, and will permit the integration of labor to be reached by every individual.''

tion in the future) ; if I were to do so, I should have to repeat what has been written by Anarchists from the time of Godwin, and what may be found, with all necessary explanations, in a whole series of books and pamphlets.

I will say only that the State is a form of social life which has developed in our European civilization, under the influence of a series of causes,* only since the end of the sixteenth century. Before the sixteenth century the State, in its Roman form, did not exist—or, more exactly, it existed only in the minds of the historians who trace the genealogy of Russian autocracy to Rurik and that of France to the Merovingian kings.

Furthermore, the State (State-Justice, State-Church, State-Army) and Capitalism are, in our opinion, inseparable concepts. In history these institutions developed side by side, mutually supporting and reenforcing each other. They are bound together, not by a mere coincidence of contemporaneous development, but by the bond of cause and effect, effect and cause. Thus, the State appears to us as a society for the mutual insurance of the landlord, the warrior, the judge, and the priest, constituted in order

---

*An analysis of which may be found—say—in the pamphlet, "The State and its Historic Role" (*Freedom* pamphlets).

to enable every one of them to assert his respective authority over the people and to exploit the poor. To contemplate the destruction of Capitalism without the abolition of the State—though the latter was created solely for the purpose of fostering Capitalism and has grown up alongside of it—is just as absurd, in our opinion, as it is to hope that the emancipation of the laborer will be accomplished through the action of the Christian church or of Cæsarism. Many socialists of the thirties and forties, and even the fifties, hoped for this; but for us, who have entered upon the twentieth century, it is ridiculous to cherish such hopes as this!

X.

It is obvious that, since Anarchism differs so widely in its method of investigation and in its fundamental principles, alike from the academical sociologists and from its social-democratic fraternity, it must of necessity differ from them all in its means of action.

Understanding Law, Right, and the State as we do, we cannot see any guarantee of progress, still less of a social revolution, in the submission of the Individual to the State. We are therefore no longer able to say, as do the superficial interpreters of social phenomena, that modern Capitalism has come into being through "the anarchy of exploitation," through "the theory of non-interference," which—we are told—the States have carried out by practicing the formula of "let them do as they like" (*laissez faire, laissez passer*). We know that this is not true. While giving the capitalist any degree of free scope to amass his wealth at the expense of the helpless laborers, the government has NOWHERE and NEVER during the whole nineteenth century afforded the laborers the opportunity "to do as they pleased." The terrible revolutionary, that is, Jacobinist, convention legislated: "For strikes, for forming a State within the State—death!" In 1813 people were hanged in England for going out on strike, and in 1831 they were deported to Australia for forming the Great Trades' Union (Union of all Trades) of Robert Owen; in the sixties people were still condemned to hard labor for participating in strikes, and even now, in 1902, trade unions are prosecuted for damages amounting to half a million dollars for picketing—for having dissuaded laborers from working in times of strike. What is one to say, then, of France, Belgium, Switzerland (remember the massacre at Airolo!), and especially of Germany and Russia? It is needless, also, to tell how, by means of taxes, the State brings laborers to the verge of poverty which puts them body and soul in the power of the factory boss; how the communal lands have been robbed from the people, and are still robbed from them in England by means of the Enclosure Acts. Or, must we remind the reader how, even at the present moment, all the States, without exception, are creating directly (what is the use of talking of "the original accumulation" when it is continued at the present time!) all kinds of monopolies—in railroads, tramways, telephones, gasworks, waterworks, electric works, schools, etc., etc. In short, the system of non-interference—the *laissez faire*—has never been applied for one single hour by any government. And therefore, if it is permissible for middle-class economists to affirm that the system of "non-interference" is practiced (since they endeavor to prove that poverty is a law of nature), it is simply shameful that socialists should speak thus to the workers. *Freedom to oppose exploitation has so far never and nowhere existed.* Everywhere it had to be taken by force, step by step, at the cost of countless sacrifices. "Non-interference," and more than non-interference—direct support; help and protection—existed *only* in the interests of the exploiters. *Nor could it be otherwise.* The mission of the Church has been to hold the people in intellectual slavery; the mission of the State was to hold them, half starved, in economic slavery.

Knowing this, we cannot see a guarantee of

progress in a still greater submission of all to the State. We seek progress in the fullest emancipation of the Individual from the authority of the State ; in the greatest development of individual initiative and in the limitation of all the governmental functions, but surely not in the extension thereof. The march forward in political institutions appears to us to consist in abolishing, in the first place, the State authority which has fixed itself upon society (especially since the sixteenth century), and which now tries to extend its functions more and more ; and, in the second place, in allowing the broadest possible development for the principle of free agreement, and in acknowledging the independence of all possible associations formed for definite ends, embracing in their federations the whole of society. The life of society itself we understand, not as something complete and rigid, but as something never perfect—something ever striving for new forms, and ever changing these forms in accordance with the needs of the time. This is what *life* is in Nature.

Such a conception of human progress and of what we think desirable in the future (what, in our opinion, can increase the sum of happiness) leads us inevitably to our own special tactics in the struggle. It induces us to strive for the greatest possible development of personal initiative in every individual and group, and to secure unity of action, not through discipline, but through the unity of aims and the mutual confidence which never fail to develop when a great number of persons have consciously embraced some common idea. This tendency manifests itself in all the tactics and in all the internal life of every Anarchist group, and so far we have never had the opportunity of seeing these tactics fail.

Then, we assert and endeavor to prove that it devolves upon every new economic form of social life to develop *its own* new form of political relations. It has been so in the past, and so it undoubtedly will be in the future. New forms are already germinating all round.

Feudal right and autocracy, or, at least, the almost unlimited power of a tsar or a king, have moved hand in hand in history. They depended on each other in this development. Exactly in the same way the rule of the capitalists has evolved its own characteristic political order — representative government — both in strictly centralized monarchies and in republics.

Socialism, whatever may be the form in which it will appear, and in whatever degree it may approach to its unavoidable goal—Communism, —will also have to choose *its own* form of political structure. Of the old form *it cannot make use*, no more than it could avail itself of the hierarchy of the Church or of autocracy. The State bureaucracy and centralization are as irreconcilable with Socialism as was autocracy with capitalist rule. One way or another, Socialism must become *more popular*, more communalistic, and less dependent upon indirect government through elected representatives. It must become more *self-governing*. Besides, when we closely observe the modern life of France, Spain, England, and the United States, we notice in these countries the evident tendency to form into groups of entirely independent communes, towns and villages, which would combine by means of free federation, in order to satisfy innumerable needs and attain certain immediate ends. Of course, neither the Russian Minister Witte nor the German William II, nor even the Jacobinists who to-day rule Switzerland, are making for this goal. All these work upon the old model for capitalist and governmental centralization in the hands of the State ; but the above-mentioned dismemberment of the State, both territorial and functional, is undoubtedly aimed at by the progressive part of West European society and of the American people. In actual life this tendency manifests itself in thousands of attempts at organization outside the State, fully independent of it ; as well as in attempts to take hold of various functions which had been previously usurped by the

State and which, of course, it has never properly performed. And then, as a great social phenomenon of universal import, this tendency found expression in the Paris Commune of 1871 and in a whole series of similar uprisings in France and Spain; while in the domain of thought—of ideas spreading through society—this view has already acquired the force of an extremely important factor of future history. The future revolutions in France and in Spain will be *communalist*—not centralist.

On the strength of all this, we are convinced that to work in favor of a centralized State-capitalism and to see in it a *desideratum*, means to work *against* the tendency of progress already manifest. We see in such work as this a gross misunderstanding of the historic mission of Socialism itself—a great historical mistake, and we make war upon it. To assure the laborers that they will be able to establish Socialism, or even to take the first steps on the road to Socialism, by retaining the entire government machinery, and changing only the persons who manage it; not to promote, but even to retard the day on which the working people's minds shall be bent upon discovering their own, new forms of political life,—this is in our eyes a colossal historical blunder which borders upon crime.

Finally, since we represent a revolutionary party, we try to study the history of the origin and development of past revolutions. We endeavor, first of all, to free the histories of revolutions written up till now from the partisan, and for the most part false, governmental coloring that has been given them. In the histories hitherto written we do not yet see *the people;* nor do we see how revolutions began. The stereotyped phrases about the desperate condition of people previous to revolutions, fail to explain whence, amid this desperation, came the hope of something better—whence came the revolutionary spirit. And therefore, after reading these histories, we put them aside, and, going back to first sources, try to learn from them what caused the people to rise and what was its part in revolutions.

Thus, we understand the Great French Revolution not at all as it is pictured by Louis Blanc, who presents it chiefly as a great political movement directed by the Jacobin Club. We see in it, first of all, a chaotic *popular* movement, chiefly of the peasant folk ("Every village had its Robespierre," as the Abbé Grégoire, who *knew* the people's revolt, remarked to the historian Schlosser). This movement aimed chiefly at the destruction of every vestige of *feudal rights* and of the redemptions that had been imposed for the abolition of some of them, as well as at the recovery of the *lands* which had been seized from the village communes by vultures of various kinds. And in so far the peasant movement was successful. Then, upon this foundation of revolutionary tumult, of increased pulsation of life, and of disorganization of all the powers of the State, we find, on the one hand, developing amongst the town laborers a tendency towards a vaguely understood socialist equality ; and, on the other hand, the middle classes working hard, and successfully, in order to establish their own authority upon the ruins of that of royalty and nobility. To this end the middle classes fought stubbornly and desperately that they might create a powerful, all-inclusive, centralized government, which would preserve and assure to them their right of property (gained partly by plunder before and during the Revolution) and afford them the full opportunity of exploiting the poor without any legal restrictions. This power, this right to exploit, the middle classes really obtained ; and in the State centralization which was created by the revolutionary Jacobinists, Napoleon found an excellent soil for establishing his empire. From this centralized authority, which kills all local life, France is suffering even to this very day, and the first attempt to throw off its yoke— an attempt which opened a new era in history— was made by the proletariat of Paris only in 1871.

Without entering here upon an analysis of other revolutionary movements, it is sufficient to say that we understand the coming social revolution, not at all as a Jacobinist dictatorship— not at all as a reform of the social institutions by means of laws issued by a Convention or a Senate or a Dictator. Such revolutions have never occurred, and a movement which should take this form would be doomed to inevitable death. We understand the revolution as a widespread popular movement, during which, in every town and village within the region of the revolt, the masses will have to take upon themselves the task of rebuilding society—will have to take up themselves *the work of construction upon communistic bases*, without awaiting any orders and directions from above; that is, first of all, they will have to organize, one way or another, the means of supplying food to everyone and of providing dwellings for all, and then produce whatever will be found necessary for feeding, clothing, and sheltering everybody.

As to the representative government, whether self-appointed or elected—be it "the dictatorship of the proletariat," as they said in the forties in France and are still saying in Germany, or an elected "temporary government," or, again, a Jacobinist "convention,"—we place in it no hopes whatever. Not because we personally do not like it, but because nowhere and

86

never in history do we find that people, carried into government by a revolutionary wave, have proved equal to the occasion; always and everywhere they have fallen *below* the revolutionary requirements of the moment; always and everywhere they became an obstacle to the revolution. We place no hope in this representation because, in the work of rebuiding society upon new communist principles, separate individuals, however wise and devoted to the cause, are and must be powerless. They can only find a legal expression for such a destruction as is already being accomplished—at most they can but widen and extend that destruction so as to *suggest* it to regions which have not yet begun it. But that is all. The destruction must be wrought from below in every portion of the territory; otherwise it will not be done. To impose it by law is impossible, as, indeed, the revolt of the Vendée has proved. As for any new bases of life which are only growing as yet,—no government can ever find an expression for them before they become defined by the constructive activity of the masses themselves, at thousands of points at once.

Looking upon the problems of the revolution in this light, Anarchism, obviously, cannot take a sympathetic attitude toward the programme which aims at "the conquest of power in present society"—*la conquête des pouvoirs*, as it is expressed in France. We know that by peaceful, parliamentary means, in the present State such a conquest as this is impossible. In proportion as the socialists become a power in the present bourgeois society and State, their Socialism must die out; otherwise the middle classes, which are much more powerful both intellectually and numerically than is admitted in the socialist press, will not recognize them as their rulers. And we know also that, were a revolution to give France or England or Germany a socialist government, the respective government would be absolutely powerless without the activity of the people themselves, and that, necessarily, it would soon begin to act fatally as a bridle upon the revolution.

Finally, our studies of the preparatory stages of all revolutions bring us to the conclusion that not a single revolution has originated in parliaments or in any other representative assembly. *All began with the people.* And no revolution has appeared in full armor—born, like Minerva out of the head of Jupiter, in a day. They all had their periods of incubation, during which the masses were very slowly becoming imbued with the revolutionary spirit, grew bolder, commenced *to hope*, and step by step emerged from their former indifference and resig-

nation. And the awakening of the revolutionary spirit always took place in such a manner
that, at first, single individuals, deeply moved
by the existing state of things, protested against
it, one by one. Many perished—"uselessly,"
the arm-chair critic would say; but the indifference of society was shaken by these progeni-
tors. The dullest and most narrow-minded
people were compelled to reflect,—Why should
men, young, sincere, and full of strength, sacri-
fice their lives in this way? It was impossible
to remain indifferent—it was necessary to take
a stand, for or against : thought was awakening.
Then, little by little, small groups came to be
imbued with the same spirit of revolt; they also
rebelled—sometimes in the hope of local success—in strikes or in small revolts against
some official whom they disliked, or in order to
get food for their hungry children, but frequently
also without any hope of success : simply because the conditions grew unbearable. Not
one, or two, or tens, but *hundreds* of similar
revolts have preceded *and must precede* every
revolution. Without these no revolution was
ever wrought; not a single concession was ever
made by the ruling classes. Even the famous
"peaceful" abolition of serfdom in Russia, of
which Tolstoy often speaks as of a peaceful
conquest, was forced upon the government by a
series of peasant uprisings, beginning with the

early fifties (perpaps as an echo of the European revolution of 1848), spreading from year to year, and gaining in importance so as to attain proportions hitherto unknown, until 1857. Alexander Herzen's words, "Better to abolish serfdom from above than to wait until the abolition comes from below,"—repeated by Alexder II before the serf-owners of Moscow—were not mere phrases, but answered to the real state of affairs. This was all the more true as to the eve of every revolution. Hundreds of partial revolts preceded every one of them. And it may be stated as a general rule that the character of every revolution is determined by the character and the aim of the uprisings by which it is preceded.

To wait, therefore, for a *social* revolution to come as a birthday present, without a whole series of protests on the part of the individual conscience, and without hundreds of preliminary revolts, by which the very nature of the revolution is determined, is, to say the least, absurd. But to assure the working people that they will gain all the benefits of a socialist revolution by confining themselves to electoral agitation, and to attack vehemently every act of individual revolt and all minor preliminary mass-revolts—even when they appear among nations historically far more revolutionary than the Germans—means to become as great an obstacle to the development of the revolutionary spirit and to all progress as was and is the Christian Church.

Without entering into further discussion of the principles of Anarchism and the Anarchist programme of action, enough has been said, I think, to show the place of Anarchism among the modern sociological sciences.

Anarchism is an attempt to apply to the study of the human institutions the generalizations gained by means of the natural-scientific inductive method; and an attempt to foresee the future steps of mankind on the road to liberty, equality, and fraternity, with a view to realizing the greatest sum of happiness for every unit of human society.

It is the inevitable result of that natural-scientific, intellectual movement which began at the close of the eighteenth century, was hampered for half a century by the reaction that set in throughout Europe after the French Revolution, and has been appearing again in full vigor ever since the end of the fifties. Its roots lie in the natural-scientific philosophy of the century mentioned. Its complete scientific basis, however, it could receive only after that awakening of naturalism which, about forty years ago, brought into being the natural-scientific study of human social institutions.

In Anarchism there is no room for those pseudo-scientific laws with which the German metaphysicians of the twenties and thirties had to content themselves. Anarchism does not recognize any method other than the natural-scientific. This method it applies to all the so-called humanitarian sciences, and, availing itself of this method as well as of all researches which have recently been called forth by it, Anarchism endeavors to reconstruct all the sciences dealing with man, and to revise every current idea of right, justice, etc., on the bases which have served for the revision of all natural sciences. Its object is to form a scientific concept of the universe embracing the whole of Nature and including Man.

This world-concept determines the position Anarchism has taken in practical life. In the struggle between the Individual and the State, Anarchism, like its predecessors of the eighteenth century, takes the side of the Individual as against the State, of Society as against the Authority which oppresses it. And, availing itself of the historical data collected by modern science, it has shown that the State—whose sphere of authority there is now a tendency among its admirers to increase, and a tendency to limit in actual life—is, in reality, a superstructure,—as harmful as it is unnecessary, and, for us Europeans, of a comparatively recent origin ; a superstructure in the interests of Capitalism—

agrarian, industrial, and financial—which in ancient history caused the decay (relatively speaking) of politically-free Rome and Greece, and which caused the death of all other despotic centers of civilization of the East and of Egypt. The power which was created for the purpose of welding together the interests of the landlord, the judge, the warrior, and the priest, and has been opposed throughout history to every attempt of mankind to create for themselves a more assured and freer mode of life,— this power cannot become an instrument for emancipation, any more than Cæsarism (Imperialism) or the Church can become the instrument for a social revolution.

In the economic field, Anarchism has come to the conclusion that the root of modern evil lies, not in the fact that the capitalist appropriates the profits or the surplus-value, but in the very possibility of these profits, which accrue only because millions of people have literally nothing to subsist upon without selling their labor-power at a price which makes profits and the creation of "surplus values" possible. Anarchism understands, therefore, that in political economy attention must be directed first of all to so-called "consumption," and that the first concern of the revolution must be to reorganize that so as to provide food, clothing and shelter for all. "Production," on the other hand, must be so adapted as to satisfy this primary, fundamental need of society. Therefore, Anarchism cannot see in the next coming revolution a mere exchange of monetary symbols for labor-checks, or an exchange of present Capitalism for State-capitalism. It sees in it the first step on the road to No-government Communism.

Whether or not Anarchism is right in its conclusions, will be shown by a scientific criticism of its bases and by the practical life of the future. But in one thing it is absolutely right : in that it has included the study of social institutions in the sphere of natural-scientific investigations; has forever parted company with metaphysics; and makes use of the method by which modern natural science and modern material philosophy were developed. Owing to this, the very mistakes which Anarchism may have made in its researches can be detected the more readily. But its conclusions can be verified only by the same natural-scientific, inductive-deductive method by which every science and every scientific concept of the universe is created.

Made in the USA
Columbia, SC
20 February 2024